Hello, America!

Martin Luther King, Jr. Memorial

by Katherine Rawson

Bullfrog
Books

Ideas for Parents and Teachers

Bullfrog Books let children practice reading informational text at the earliest reading levels. Repetition, familiar words, and photo labels support early readers.

Before Reading

- Discuss the cover photo. What does it tell them?
- Look at the picture glossary together. Read and discuss the words.

Read the Book

- "Walk" through the book and look at the photos. Let the child ask questions. Point out the photo labels.
- Read the book to the child, or have him or her read independently.

After Reading

- Prompt the child to think more. Ask: What do you know about Dr. Martin Luther King, Jr.? What more would you like to learn about him?

Bullfrog Books are published by Jump!
5357 Penn Avenue South
Minneapolis, MN 55419
www.jumplibrary.com

Library of Congress Cataloging-in-Publication Data

Names: Rawson, Katherine, author.
Title: Martin Luther King, Jr. Memorial / by Katherine Rawson.
Description: Minneapolis, MN: Jump!, Inc., 2018.
Series: Hello, America! | Includes index.
Audience: K–3. | Audience: 5–8.
Identifiers: LCCN 2017023547 (print)
LCCN 2017024363 (ebook)
ISBN 9781624966613 (e-book)
ISBN 9781620318706 (hard cover: alk. paper)
Subjects: LCSH: Martin Luther King, Jr., Memorial (Washington, D.C.)—Juvenile literature.
Memorials—Washington (D.C.)—Juvenile literature.
Classification: LCC F203.4.M118 (ebook)
LCC F203.4.M118 R39 2017 (print) | DDC 975.3—dc23
LC record available at https://lccn.loc.gov/2017023547

Editor: Kirsten Chang
Book Designer: Molly Ballanger
Photo Researcher: Molly Ballanger

Photo Credits: Julie Clopper/Shutterstock, cover; Lissandra Melo/Shutterstock, 1, 20–21; Ariel Skelley/Getty, 3; naluwan/Shutterstock, 4 (foreground); Stephen Therres/Shutterstock, 4 (background); Brandon Bourdages/Shutterstock, 5; f11photo/Shutterstock, 6–7, 23tr; Walter Bennett/Getty, 8; William Lovelace/Getty, 9, 23tl; The Washington Post/Getty, 10–11, 23bl; Steve Heap/Shutterstock, 12–13, 23br; Orhan Cam/Shutterstock, 14; annebaek/iStock, 15; Pigprox/Shutterstock, 16–17; Brendan Smialowski/Stringer/Getty, 18–19; Evgeniia Ozerkina/Shutterstock, 22; TonyBaggett/iStock, 24.

Printed in the United States of America at Corporate Graphics in North Mankato, Minnesota.

SEPTEMBER 2018

Table of Contents

Words of Hope

Who is that?

Dr. Martin Luther King, Jr.

This is his memorial.

It is in Washington, D.C.

OUT OF THE MOUNTAIN OF DESPAIR,
A STONE OF HOPE

Who was Dr. King?

8

He led the civil rights movement.

He spoke.

He inspired people.

This place honors him.

See the stones?

They are tall.

They stand for struggle.

statue

Look!
Here is a statue.
It is of Dr. King.
Wow! It is tall.

It gives us hope.

15

See the wall?

It has words.

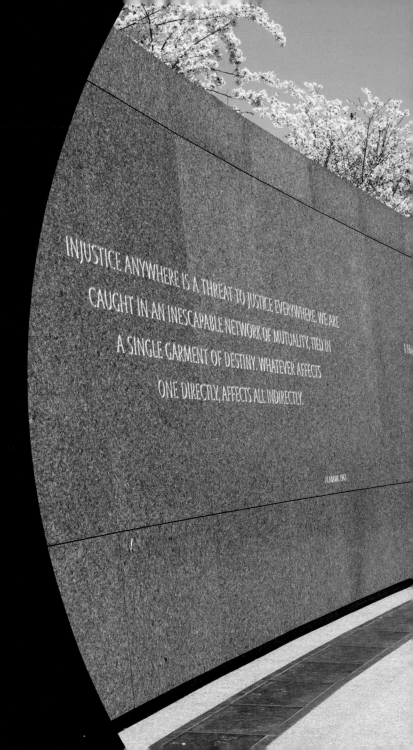

INJUSTICE ANYWHERE IS A THREAT TO JUSTICE EVERYWHERE. WE ARE
CAUGHT IN AN INESCAPABLE NETWORK OF MUTUALITY, TIED IN
A SINGLE GARMENT OF DESTINY. WHATEVER AFFECTS
ONE DIRECTLY, AFFECTS ALL INDIRECTLY.

ALABAMA, 1963

HAVE THE AUDACITY TO BE

HAVE THREE MEALS A DA

CULTURE FOR THEIR

AND FREE

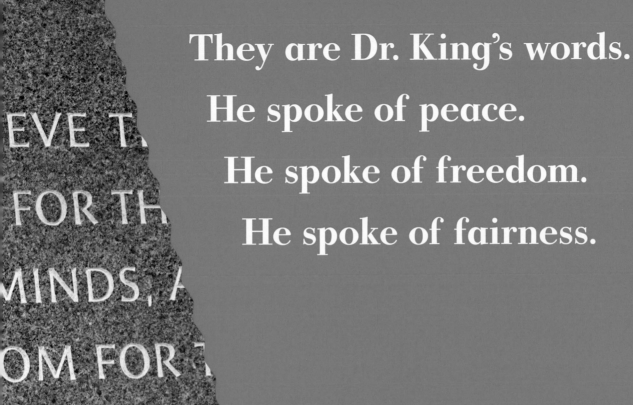

They are Dr. King's words.

He spoke of peace.

He spoke of freedom.

He spoke of fairness.

We remember him.

Parts of the Memorial

Stone of Hope

Mountain of Despair

Inscription Wall

Picture Glossary

civil rights movement
An effort by African Americans to get equal rights.

memorial
A place meant to help remember a person or event.

inspired
Encouraged and made someone feel confident and eager to do something.

struggle
A long, hard fight to get freedom or rights.

Index

To Learn More

Learning more is as easy as 1, 2, 3.

1) Go to www.factsurfer.com

2) Enter "MLKMemorial" into the search box.

3) Click the "Surf" button to see a list of websites.

With factsurfer.com, finding more information is just a click away.